# Circling Silence

*poems by*

# Laurie Wilcox-Meyer

*Finishing Line Press*
Georgetown, Kentucky

# Circling Silence

Copyright © 2018 by Laurie Wilcox-Meyer
ISBN 978-1-63534-403-5 First Edition
All rights reserved under International and Pan-American Copyright Conventions.
No part of this book may be reproduced in any manner whatsoever without written permission from the publisher, except in the case of brief quotations embodied in critical articles and reviews.

ACKNOWLEDGMENTS

Poems in this collection have been published in the following periodicals:

*Kakalak* 2015, "Citizen Dream," Slightly different version
*The Great Smokies Review* 2014, "Bedroom Wall"
*Yin Yang, A Prose and Poetry Anthology* 2016, "Remembering the Difference"

Thank you to all my teachers and to Dee, Kim, Joseph, and Sue of the Table Rock group. J, I'm forever grateful.

Publisher: Leah Maines
Editor: Christen Kincaid
Cover Art: Sesshū Tōyō
Author Photo: James Baley
Cover Design: Elizabeth Maines McCleavy

Printed in the USA on acid-free paper.
Order online: www.finishinglinepress.com
also available on amazon.com

Author inquiries and mail orders:
Finishing Line Press
P. O. Box 1626
Georgetown, Kentucky 40324
U. S. A.

# Table of Contents

Citizen Dream ............................................................. 1
Gift in Question .......................................................... 2
As One ...................................................................... 3
Gray Whales of the Bay ............................................. 4
Bedroom Wall ............................................................ 5
Barred Owl ................................................................. 6
Autumn Speak ........................................................... 7
A Way To Be .............................................................. 8
His Sundown Syndrome ............................................ 9
In the Seed ............................................................... 10
Into ........................................................................... 11
Once ......................................................................... 12
Out of the Blue ......................................................... 13
Remembering the Difference .................................. 14
Tree Talk .................................................................. 15
Snake, ...................................................................... 16
Symbiosis ................................................................. 17
Time Out .................................................................. 18
Flying Blue ............................................................... 19
Tunnel of Love ......................................................... 20
Twos ......................................................................... 21
Wild .......................................................................... 22
Louisiana December ................................................ 23
The Waters of a Cajun Dream ................................. 24
Yield ......................................................................... 25

"The greatest human discoveries in the future will be the discovery of human intimacy with all those other modes of being that live with us on this planet, inspire our art and literature, reveal that numinous world whence all things come into being, and with which we exchange the very substance of life."
.....Thomas Berry (from *The Great Work*)

## Citizen Dream
*Persistent is the peace that dreams itself.*

I am the fermata.
A stone body fermata not long enough to forgive.
A crescendo wave.   A swell.   A sea disturbed…
Who will rock my legs to sleep?
Clever moon   why are you so silent?
A bullfrog drones from the cypress bog.
Remnant-womb of the human brain
gifting a lone monk sounding his shruti box.
An unfigured continuo.
Measures unmeasured.
Again.   Again…the public moves hand-in-hand.
What-is-mutual chimes from the wild preserve.
Finally unfurling its cosmic song.

**Gift In Question**

If I send my friend a book, more trees will be cut down.
I'll gift an e-book.  It'll fly through the i-cloud to reach her.
Still, she'll feel the dark, smooth words.

Perhaps, someday soon
there will be a "vacant" sign at the bookstore.
These are late times.
We move slowly like the clouds we walk through.

## As One

Ancient limestone landscape
intimate with the sea
receives the sky raining down its wine
as shades of green
where gravity warps an invisible mesh between
and within an earshot's echo of light.
Outside the lines
in shadows of vowels
soothing night,
two lovers rest
in true conversation.

**Gray Whales of the Bay**

Waves of gray grace.
Migrating.

Arch to dive
deeper.
Barnacle-tail, your fingerprint,

slips into the Baja lagoon.
Your liquid footprint lilts,
a circling silence.

I wait for what moves.
A cloud of breath—no breach,
no fin-slap, no head-raise to spy.

Forty-ton mother, one-ton calf
and escort
make passage of three.

She pumps her fat milk into
her ton-baby—twelve month gestation.
Magic cream.

Dark world of Magdalena Bay
is a birthing ground.
Call me Magdalena.

I drive my car to shop for food.
My children's meals come from a box.

## Bedroom Wall

You stuff aluminum foil inside the hole
the copperhead entered
because you chased the snake
into your bedroom.

Rising dust, red tears in the air,
barefoot with child on the way.
Each night before you sleep, you ask
*is serpent there?*

The child turns, glistening,
practiced in the dark.
Snake dreams itself into a bird.

Ancient blue light of a mountain view,
shines on a rocker, calm and true.

**Barred Owl**

Out my kitchen window, the hummingbird's black tongue flickers in delight.
I mince the garlic, chop an onion, splash Tabasco for fire.

Three times I hear owl's couplet,
Song in shadow:

   *Who cooks for you?*
   *Who cooks for youuuu?*

Majestic thief of otherworldly flights
I am served by you.

**Autumn Speak**

The river slides over boulders.

Granite edges point to tip the stern

and bow of our canoe.

Red leaves walk on water.

**A Way To Be**


Not seeing their black-brilliant-bodies,
I listen to crows quibble in the trees.
Coming to words here and there.
Leaving the rest pure.
Like the maple leaf dangling
   by spider's invisible haze.
      Waving midair    without care.

The leaf   is dance   is gift   is life.
The center of the world    anywhere.

**His Sundown Syndrome**


He's 90 years old.
I bring him cake in the early morning.

The same day at 5pm, he's 80.
He sings a measure or two, *Carmina Burana, O Fortuna.*

Now 70 at 5:05 pm, lamenting his past.
Barehanded, he reaches in the oven for a roll.

60 at 5:10 pm.
He can't find fresh butter in the bedroom nightstand.

50 at 5:15 pm.
Silence.

It is 5:30. He is Rumi's empty garlic.
And cannot see the fig tree or the garden.

**In The Seed**

Upon this table
a book—
pages
trees
sun
rain.
Grasses
govern us—
their cell by cell
tells us to eat.
And by eating
we are eaten.

The grasses grow tall.

**Into**

Decades ago, we would put a friend in the trunk of my car
to pay less for the drive-in movie.

Now, this friend dreams of an Indian man
conducting a train that will always sail joyfully through walls.

Sparrow, take me to your home of grass, snakeskin, spider eggs,
sticks, and string.
The nesting site stolen from a Carolina wren.

**Once**

There was a time when owls perched
on the backs of black bears.
Rambling together,
cooling even the sun.
In paradise—animals reading our hearts
were never afraid.
Holly trees smooth like French silk.
Sharp words
dissolving on my tongue.
Heat of my mind
melting.

**Out of the Blue**

Why did Mother wade in her nerves when I was four?
It was only my sandal floating downstream.
Decades later I can still hear the rhododendron sighs.
Now, Great Blue heron balances its weight
on a one-legged stance.
Smoke-gray curves.  The down, ash-gray.
On a wooden bridge, he and I are hand in hand.
It is there love whispers.
We see the jeweled fingerlings weightless in the stream.

**Remembering the Difference**

If I see only a beast in every moment,
my breath, once a shapeshifter, evaporates to bone dry.
A mirage will live in me.

Blind to the acorn, oak's gem,
I'd brook nothing wild.

Back at square one and our driveway's chalked game
of Four Square, with the dime store's red ball,
the game plays me.
The saint of every moment.

## Tree Talk

Her grandfather dug the hole wider
to rescue her black lab retriever
out from the muck.
As he worked, she saw the white mycelium.
Then the red and yellow mineral horizons.
Imagined the pathways underground
out from where the stand of trees
bloomed a single green crown.
She fell in love with the soil
after her dog fell into the outhouse pit.
Years later she would study forestry.
Her working lab:
hours
in a car
to wait out Louisiana black bears
in hopes her isotopes
planted
would sound
from certain tree trunks.
She found that mother trees
would feed their kith and kin.
And others into distance.
Cohesive talk
colonized by fungus
and the roots.
Quiet.
Intimate in the dark.
Transporting only what was needed.
Redemption.
Discounting wonder.

**Snake,**

I have found you on this road
after the fact of,
and to be more than,
your pink lung resting on asphalt.
Yes, my car crushed you.
But I thought you were just some red-black rope.

You splay tiny patterns.  A mandala
in slow-glowing green ribbon and rose.
More than all the grains of sand.
Radiant.
It's strange, now, how easy on my eyes
is the unchosen landing where you lay,
hidden in stillness.

**Symbiosis**

A painter glides gray pigment onto her canvas.
The way lichens grow from both fungi and algae
while clinging to a tree.
Or on a fallen limb.

**Time Out**

Not just the bougainvillea on vacation
but the ancient palms now in view,
the philodendron being in the living room,
the broken light to our dark corners.

What is this hurried waltz we do?
All important selves in march of triple time,
measures meter monkey mind.
Racing! Stomping! Crashing! into
also dense projections—
We sting with our vibrations!

Bonsai's miniature presence—vast and timeless
as childhood plays under saris of Spanish moss,
as celestial space in a doll's house,
as bicycles at the speed of light,
as boundless hide and seek in a field,
in a barn packed with hay
and the needle tossed aside
for another day.

**Flying Blue**
    *For Bill Evans*

I suppose the pianist took one-too-many music theory classes.
Made him want to graduate real quick
into Crescent City humidity,
or New Orleans where the real jazz juts from Absinthe bars,
swirling for wonderland up and away from terrestrial life.
Because bent notes melt on Bourbon Street.
Mid-afternoon like midnight.
Melodies the silken whispers on tongues.
On hearts.
The French Quarter streetlights are also Rubenesque.
Wet light lifts from cobblestones.
O! Icarus of the black and white keys, No wink
or word could tell you not to fly too high.
Smack needles before, during, after
and by the piano's pedal
at the end.

I can still hear his gone notes flying in air.
Maniacal magic into the midnight.
His wild limbs completely at ease.

**Tunnel of Love**

I crawl under the dining table with my granddaughter
"playing hide and seek."
Her squeal reminds me
of found treasure.
Two of us in a cave
reading a book about a train.
Page after page.
What whispers from the railroad tunnel?
*There…* a puff of steam.
A voice says to say it in English,
yet I crawl hand by hand,
toward this love
on the tracks.
A full moon revealing
our eyes.

**Twos**

Two tree trunks.

Two woodpeckers in sync.

Too, that he gathers kindling for his home fire.

To the chef knowing fire as feminine.

To their love-food in the oven.

To those in joy.

To the sounds in the flames of their fire.  Like a Festival.

**Wild**

The glacial crawls are regressing.
We're fueling an errant thief.
It's ice we require in our fire of fire.
Chill the landslides and for a while
let the red glow be.

Hear the offbeat pulse in the wild.
Its genes barely move.
Hardly an ember.
Near impotent, it pales in reverse.

Fire said to ice,
Love   love   love.
And ice agreed.

## Louisiana December

Fatwood sizzles in the fireplace.
Sparks our gray dissolve.
Karo, butter, bourbon,
two cups of pecans in a pie crust.
Gas oven breathes orange-blue.
White walls of knotty pine close in.
Near the laundry closet gridlock.

A stranger knocks on the back door.
In the left pocket of his coat
a squirrel—dressed, wrapped in plastic.
*"Best in a stew. Two dollars would do."*
Is the squirrel's tail in his back pocket for good luck?
Once, in Ponchatoula, I saw a man
pin a fuzzy tail onto the back of his blue overalls.
What animal was he wishing to be?

I moved far away from my first-home.
Chicago.
Squirrels up north also remember
where all the nuts are buried.

**The Waters of a Cajun Dream**

He knows Louisiana green.
The Purple Pitcher plants
and Venus Flytraps that swallow flies
so the Atchafalaya Basin blooms.
Yet still there's warmer earth.
An ocean in his eyes.
Where the dreams of dolphins
friendly to owl flicker.
What sends me into a moon glisten
of all colors seen and unseen.
I could never have imagined
such fertile silk waters.

**Yield**

I am not loyal to suffering.
Hear the trees sway?
A circular economy chimes.
Floating laughter.
I whistle for a hawk…..Carry me
to Michelangelo's ceiling frescoes.
There up high the painter once crouched in pain.
I draw open the curtains covering his art.
Joy leaps out from sorrow.
Heaven works in reverse.

Laurie Wilcox-Meyer lives in the mountains of Western North Carolina, where she often spots bears while hiking and meditating about her next poem. Her poems have appeared in *The Great Smokies Review, Kakalak, Artemis Journal, Wild Goose Poetry Review,* and *Birdsong Anthology.*

www.ingramcontent.com/pod-product-compliance
Lightning Source LLC
LaVergne TN
LVHW041515070426
835507LV00012B/1589